Troy

UNEARTHING ANCIENT WORLDS

Ann Kerns

Twenty-First Century Books • Minneapolis

For Jeffrey

Twenty-First Century Books
A division of Lerner Publishing Group, Inc.
241 First Avenue North
Minneapolis, MN 55401 U.S.A.

Website address: www.lernerbooks.com

Library of Congress Cataloging-in-Publication Data

Kerns, Ann, 1959–
    Troy / by Ann Kerns.
        p.   cm. — (Unearthing ancient worlds)
    Includes bibliographical references and index.
    ISBN 978–0–8225–7582–5 (lib. bdg. : alk. paper)
    1. Schliemann, Heinrich, 1822–1890—Juvenile literature. 2. Troy (Extinct city)—Juvenile literature. 3. Excavations (Archaeology)—Turkey—Troy (Extinct city)—Juvenile literature. 4. Archaeologists—Germany—Biography—Juvenile literature. 5. Greece—Civilization—To 146 B.C.—Juvenile literature. 6. Civilization, Mycenaean—Juvenile literature. I. Title.
    DF212.S4K47 2009
    939'.21—dc22   2007042903

Manufactured in the United States of America
1 2 3 4 5 6 – PA – 14 13 12 11 10 09

TABLE OF CONTENTS

This painting depicts Menelaus *(center)* and Helen *(left)* reunited after the destruction of Troy. It appears on a large vase and was created by a Greek artist around 345 B.C.

INTRODUCTION

About 1200 B.C., according to legend, one thousand ships gathered in the Greek port of Aulis. Each ship was filled with Greek warriors. At a favorable sign from the gods, the ships set sail across the Aegean Sea. They were bound for Troy, a city on the western edge of Asia Minor (in present-day Turkey).

Paris, a prince from Troy, had stolen Helen, the wife of a Greek king named Menelaus. Menelaus was enraged that the Trojans refused to return Helen. He turned to his brother, Agamemnon (also a king), for help. Together they had raised an enormous army. This army's destruction of Troy became one of the most famous stories in history.

The Trojan War took place during a historical period called the Bronze Age. In the region surrounding the Aegean Sea, the Bronze Age lasted from about 3200 to 1100 B.C. During this period and for long after, the ancient Greeks did not record their stories in writing. Stories were passed on by oral tradition—the reciting of poems and the singing of songs. Oral stories of the Trojan War must have been very important to the Greeks, because they lasted for centuries. One person who heard the stories sometime in the 700s or 800s B.C. was a young Greek boy named Homer.

When Homer grew up, he became an *aoidos*, a poet who sang his poetry. His most famous and popular poems were about the Trojan War. As

Homer grew older, writing became more common in Greece. Homer's followers recorded his knowledge of Trojan War oral tradition in two written poems, *The Iliad* and *The Odyssey*. Both are epic poems—long works about heroes and important events. Most of what we in modern times know of the Trojan War comes from these epics.

This marble bust of Homer is an eighteenth-century copy of a first-century B.C. statue.

THE JUDGMENT OF PARIS

Greek mythology tells us the background of the kidnapping of Helen. Three goddesses—Hera, Athena, and Aphrodite—asked Paris to choose the fairest among them. Each goddess promised Paris something if he chose her. Hera, the queen of the gods, promised Paris that he would be the ruler over all Asia. Athena, the goddess of wisdom, promised to make Paris wise and unbeatable in war. Aphrodite, the goddess of love, promised Paris the love of Helen, the world's most beautiful woman. Paris decided that Aphrodite was the fairest goddess.

Aphrodite and Paris plotted to capture Helen. Paris pretended to make a friendly visit to Menelaus at his palace in Amyklai in southern Greece. When Menelaus was called away suddenly on royal business, Paris ran off with his wife.

Whether Helen was taken against her will is unclear. Some ancient Greek sources say that she did not want to go with Paris. Other sources, such as Homer, say she and Paris fell in love while he visited Menelaus. She willingly ran away with him. Whatever the case, Helen ended up in Troy with Paris.

WAR CLOUDS GATHER

News reached Menelaus that his wife was gone. He went immediately to his older brother, Agamemnon. Agamemnon was the head of the family known as the House of Atreus. He was a powerful king who ruled most of southern Greece from his palace in Mycenae. He agreed with his brother that Helen's kidnapping was an outrage.

Agamemnon and Menelaus had many allies throughout the Greek isles. They called upon those allies to join their army against the Trojans. Many of the most powerful kingdoms in the region sent large numbers of warriors to Mycenae. Some of the most famous warriors were Odysseus from Ithaca, Ajax from Salamis, and Achilles of a people called the Myrmidons.

The Greek armies that joined together under Agamemnon were called the Achaeans. When the Achaeans arrived at the bay of Troy, they docked their sleek black ships. The Achaeans set up camp in the plain between the Aegean and Troy. There they spent ten years trying to break through Troy's high city walls.

The Iliad begins in the tenth year of the war. The Achaeans were exhausted and sick. The Trojans were trapped in their own city. Then suddenly the Achaeans roused themselves for battle again. The Trojans were doomed.

THE HEROIC AGE

Between the Bronze Age and Homer's time, Greece struggled through a dark age. During a dark age, civilization declines, or begins to fail. Many factors can lead to a dark age. War, a natural disaster, or famine (a long-term loss of food sources) can all be causes. Historians are not sure what exactly led to Greece's dark age. But they do know that from about 1100 to 750

FAST FACTS ABOUT TROY

- Troy was an ancient city in the land that became modern-day Turkey.

- According to Greek legend, Troy was a rich and beautiful city.

- Legend also says that Troy was the site of a long war. During this Trojan War, Greek armies attacked Troy for ten years. They finally took over and burned the city in about 1180 B.C.

- About 800 B.C., Homer wrote about part of the Trojan War. He called his poem *The Iliad.*

- In modern times, historians were not sure exactly where Troy had stood. They could find no traces of the ancient city.

- In the A.D. 1860s, German businessperson Heinrich Schliemann began searching for Troy. He used *The Iliad* as a guide.

B.C., great Greek cities were destroyed. Trade and exchange with other peoples stopped. Art and culture collapsed.

But by the time Homer was an adult, culture, trade, and politics were all improving. Greeks wanted to forget the dark age. They looked to ancient times for the roots of their culture. They saw the Bronze Age as the "light behind the dark age." To Greeks in Homer's day, the Bronze Age was a time of heroes. They imagined the women of this period as beautiful and strong. They imagined the men as almost like the gods in their strength and bravery. Stories such as that of the Trojan War gave the Greeks heroic epics about their ancient history.

To modern eyes, the characters in *The Iliad* often seem less than heroic. Paris causes the destruction of a city simply so he can have Helen. Helen runs away from her husband and child and then is tormented by guilt. And much of *The Iliad* is concerned with a fierce quarrel between Achilles and Agamemnon, who are supposed to be on the same side.

Homer does not shy away from showing his heroes' flaws. As a warrior, Achilles is "godlike," swift, and brave. But he is driven by rage and wounded pride. Agamemnon stands among the other warriors "like a bull rising head and shoulders over the herds." Yet he is arrogant and reckless.

Homer's ability to present human flaws alongside heroic feats makes *The Iliad* more than the story of war. The details, the characters, and the emotion of *The Iliad* provide one of our best glimpses into an ancient world. Its influence on literature has lasted into modern times.

THE POWER OF *THE ILIAD*

In the 1830s, twenty-six centuries after Homer, a young boy in Germany learned the tale of the Trojan War. According to his memoirs, Heinrich Schliemann was just ten years old when his father gave him a book about Troy. As the years passed, Schliemann continued to read about Greek history. He taught himself to speak Greek.

In Schliemann's time, Greek history and culture were very popular in western Europe. People greatly admired ancient Greece. They believed Greece, like ancient Rome, represented Europe's common cultural heritage. Most people thought works such as *The Iliad*, *The Odyssey*, and *The Aeneid*

Heinrich Schliemann and the
Ancient Greek World, 1868–1890

(a Roman epic about the Trojan hero Aeneas) were historically accurate. But scholars wondered if the Troy described by Homer had ever really existed. Had any Troy ever existed? If it had, why could no one find evidence of it?

Scholars knew the general region where Troy was supposed to have stood. They knew a city had existed in the region into Roman times. They knew the city's various names from Roman documents and local traditions. Over the centuries, it had been called Ilios, Ilium, and Troia. But no one knew where it was exactly. They did not know what had happened to the beautiful walled city filled with palaces and gold that Homer described. The whereabouts of Troy was, as Schliemann said, "a great historical mystery." It was a mystery Schliemann would spend twenty years of his life determined to solve.

The Troad region covers a small peninsula on the western coast of modern-day Turkey.
The land slopes down from Mount Ida to the Aegean Sea through marshy wetlands.
Researchers believe that water levels in the area were higher when Troy was at its height.

CHAPTER one

SCHLIEMANN ARRIVES IN ANATOLIA

By the time Heinrich Schliemann arrives in the region of Asia Minor called the Troad, it is already late afternoon. But it is mid-August, and the sun is still strong and hot. The year is 1868, and this is Schliemann's first trip to the area.

The Troad is a small peninsula of Anatolia. To the west lies the Aegean Sea. In the south, Mount Ida (sacred to the Greek god Zeus) towers over the area's plains and wooded hills. Small farms dot the land around the Scamander and Simois rivers. Turks, Greeks, and other groups of people live in this area controlled by the Turkish government. It is an unremarkable region, except that it is believed to contain the ruins of one of the most famous cities in all history—Troy.

Schliemann has hired a local man to take him to the Turkish village of Bunarbashi. They have rented two horses. The sun sinks lower, but Schliemann is determined to reach Bunarbashi that day. Most of the experts he has read and talked to think that Bunarbashi probably sits atop the ruins of Troy.

SCHLIEMANN'S DREAM

Schliemann's friend Ernst Ziller recommended this trip to the Troad. Ziller is an Austrian architect living in Athens, the Greek capital. He knows of Schliemann's interest in archaeology and antiquities—the long-lost, buried remains of ancient civilizations. As a tourist, Schliemann has already visited the Great Wall of China, Japanese temples, Egyptian pyramids, and the ruins of Pompeii in Italy.

So far this summer, Schliemann has seen Ithaca, Corinth, Mycenae, and Tiryns. These cities are all famed in Greek myth and history. Schliemann has already published a book about these sites. But Ziller's talk of Troy has caught his interest. Ziller is among those who believe that Bunarbashi is the site of Troy.

He encourages Schliemann to visit Frank Calvert when he arrives in the Dardanelles (the modern-day city of Canakkale). The Dardanelles is the entry point to the Troad. It is a port city along the narrow body of water that connects the Aegean to the Sea of Marmara. Frank Calvert is British, but he and his family have lived in the Dardanelles for many years. Calvert, Ziller advises, is the best local expert on the Troad's ancient history.

Schliemann makes note of Calvert's name. But before he goes to visit the Englishman, he decides to investigate Bunarbashi on his own. Schliemann is not an archaeologist, but he has grown very interested in excavating, or digging up, a ruined site. He is an amateur with little training in excavation and identification—the careful sorting and dating of found objects. But that does not trouble him. Archaeology has only just grown into a science. Several famous ruins and treasured objects have been discovered by amateurs. Any educated gentleman with enough money and leisure time can conduct an excavation.

Schliemann has money and leisure time. But he is not what many people of his day would consider an educated gentleman. As a child, Schliemann loved learning. He dreamed of being a university scholar. But he had to quit school at fourteen to work for a living. And work he did. By his mid-thirties, he was a millionaire businessman with interests all over Europe and the Americas. At the age of forty-six, he has already retired. But his marriage to a Russian woman, Ekaterina, is an unhappy one. He

This portrait shows Heinrich Schliemann around 1866.

"I saw before me the vast plain of Troy—an image that had haunted the dreams of my early childhood."

—Heinrich Schliemann, recalling his first visit to the Troad in *Ithaca, the Peloponnese and Troy* (1869)

does not want to stay with his wife at their home in Russia. Instead, he takes up world travel and the study of antiquities.

Schliemann also wants to earn the respect of the people he has always admired—university scholars. What better way to do so, he thinks, than to discover a famous archaeological site. Schliemann may not be an educated man, but he has the means to make a name for himself.

BUNARBASHI

As he rides through the afternoon heat over the roads of the Troad, Schliemann thinks of *The Iliad*. According to Homer, Troy was a great city on a hill overlooking a vast plain. It had long, "rugged walls," "well-built towers," and an enormous entrance known as the Scaean Gate. Inside the city walls, broad streets led past houses and workshops. There was a temple to the goddess Athena and one to the god Apollo. And at the highest part of the city sat Priam's castle. *The Iliad* says that Priam had fifty sons and twelve daughters. Each of them had family living quarters within the palace.

Before the war, Troy was a peaceful and prosperous city. Priam's eldest son, Hector, was happily married to Andromache. In *The Iliad*, they have a new baby, Astyanax. Priam's wife, Hecuba, was at the center of palace home life, beloved by her daughters and daughters-in-law. Other people in the city had their own homes, families, and jobs.

But no one has ever found the ruins of this great city. Scholars and archaeologists have pinpointed Bunarbashi for several reasons. Some important features of the village match descriptions from *The Iliad*. Bunarbashi was a town in the Bronze Age, the Greek era, and Roman times, just as Troy was. Homer described Troy as an acropolis—a fortified city on top of a hill. Bunarbashi has a large hill the local people call Balli-Dagh. Homer notes that Troy had hot and cold natural springs outside its walls. Bunarbashi also has this unusual feature.

How a Horse Destroyed a City

The Greeks did finally manage to conquer Troy. In the tenth year of the war, it looked to the Trojans as though the Greeks were giving up and going back to their ships. As a symbol of their defeat, the Greeks built an enormous wooden horse as a gift for the Trojans. They put the horse outside the gates of Troy and left.

The Trojans waited and watched, but there was no further sign of the Greeks. Then, believing it would offend the gods not to accept the gift, the Trojans pulled the horse inside the city and relocked the gates. It was a fatal mistake. The horse was hollow and filled with Greek soldiers. That night, as the Trojans slept, the soldiers climbed out and unlocked the gates. The entire Greek army, which had been hiding in the hills nearby, poured into the city. The Greeks emptied Troy of its treasures and gold. They killed the Trojan men and took the Trojan women and children as slaves. As they left, they set the city on fire. The Trojan horse story gave rise to a famous saying: "Beware of Greeks bearing gifts."

The earliest known image of the Trojan horse decorates the neck of this amphora (two-handled, oval, clay jar) from Mykonos, Greece. It was made in about 640 B.C.

Schliemann is excited as he and the guide approach the village. Tomorrow he will begin digging for ruins. But the Bunarbashi that greets Schliemann puts a damper on his excitement. He finds it "a dirty village of twenty hovels [shacks]."

His guide takes him to the house where he is to stay overnight. Schliemann is shocked. "Bedbugs swarmed on the walls and the wooden bench on which I was supposed to sleep," he notes in his travel diary. "The whole place is disgustingly filthy. When I asked for milk, I was given a bowl which apparently had not been rinsed in ten years." Schliemann decides he is better off sleeping under the stars on an empty stomach.

The next morning, Schliemann finds a Greek-speaking guide. They set out to explore Bunarbashi. Schliemann climbs to the top of Balli-Dagh. He gazes at the lowlands spreading out below. If Bunarbashi is Troy, then the lowlands are the great field on which the Achaeans and the Trojans clashed in battle.

But as Schliemann looks around the area, he begins to have doubts. His initial digs do not uncover any tiles or pottery—"not the slightest sign of former human activity." Schliemann is also troubled by the natural springs. Homer notes that Troy has two springs—one hot and one cold. But Bunarbashi has more than thirty springs. Schliemann doubts that Homer would have left that detail out. Schliemann also thinks the Simois and Scamander rivers are smaller than the rivers described in *The Iliad*.

Schliemann decides to take a break from his digging and consult with Frank Calvert. Perhaps the British expert will have some information for him.

FRANK CALVERT

Schliemann arrives at the Dardanelles on August 12, 1868. He calls on the Calvert house—a beautiful stone mansion overlooking the water. Frank Calvert is a sort of diplomat. He and his two brothers represent foreign governments doing business in the busy port city. When he is not working, Calvert explores the Troad. He has been doing so for years and has published several scholarly papers on the region.

Calvert invites Schliemann to stay for dinner. Schliemann is happy to relax in the Calverts' gracious home. The rooms are filled with paintings, tapestries, and comfortable furniture. The Calverts' books and many Greek and Asian artifacts reflect the family's education and culture.

Calvert and Schliemann discuss the archaeology of the Troad. Calvert gives Schliemann his opinion on Troy. He does not believe that Bunarbashi is the site of Troy. He believes Troy is buried under a hill called Hissarlik, a little to the southeast of Bunarbashi. Hissarlik, Calvert explains, sits on a plateau about 100 feet (30 meters) above a plain. The hill of Hissarlik, Calvert says, is not a natural hill. The raised land is the result of several thousand years of rubble—several cities all piled on top of one another.

Frank Calvert bought the eastern side of the hill at Hissarlik from a local farmer. He began digging for ruins. But Calvert cannot continue his excavations. The effort to uncover a city buried for twenty centuries would cost a great deal of money. The Calvert family has run into financial problems. Calvert has had to spend his time and money helping his older brother, Frederick.

Calvert had written to the British Museum in London, England, for help. If the British Museum agreed to fund the excavation, Calvert would turn everything he found over to the museum. The museum refused. It was Calvert's last hope for excavating Hissarlik himself. But if the site is

indeed Troy, it is important for the entire field of archaeology that someone excavate it. And here in his very drawing room sits a wealthy German businessman eager to excavate something. Calvert urges Schliemann to make a trip to Hissarlik.

ON TO HISSARLIK

Two days after meeting Calvert, Schliemann goes to Hissarlik. Along with a guide and five workers, he set out at five o'clock in the morning. After a couple of hours' walk in the muggy weather, they reach Hissarlik. On the hill, Schliemann finds Calvert's interrupted excavation. He spots ancient potsherds (broken bits of pottery), marble pieces, and four marble pillars "half-buried in the soil." These clues convince Schliemann that the spot marks the remains of a once-great city. By ten o'clock, Schliemann is sure of Calvert's theory about Troy.

Schliemann immediately begins making plans to excavate Hissarlik. He believes that *The Iliad*'s Troy would have been the first city built on this site. So, he reasons, it lies at the very bottom of the pile of "ruins and debris of temples and palaces." He decides to remove the entire artificial part of the hill.

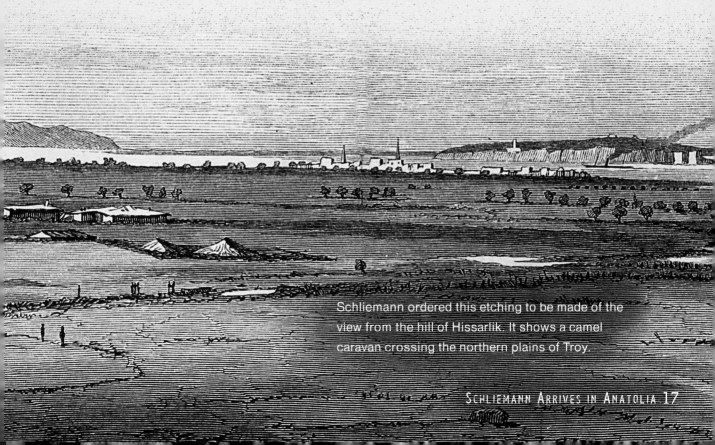

Schliemann ordered this etching to be made of the view from the hill of Hissarlik. It shows a camel caravan crossing the northern plains of Troy.

Schliemann cannot begin work right away. The weather is too hot and unhealthy. Mosquitoes from a nearby swamp carry the disease malaria. Schliemann knows he will have to wait until next spring. But he is confident that he has found his city of gold. That night he stays at an inn on a cliff overlooking the plain of what he hopes is Troy. In his diary, he records his excitement:

> When, with *The Iliad* in hand, I sat on the roof of a house and looked around me, I imagined seeing before me the fleet, camp, and assemblies of the Greek; Troy and its Pergamus fortress on the plateau of Hissarlik; troops marching to and fro and battling each other in the lowland between city and camp. For two hours the main events of *The Iliad* passed before my eyes until darkness and violent hunger forced me to leave the roof.

Fortified Cities

Most of the Bronze Age kingdoms throughout the Greek mainland and islands were fortified cities. To fortify, or protect, his city, a king usually built it high on a hill. That position made it harder for enemies to suddenly attack. High, thick walls enclosed the city. The palace and other important buildings were inside these walls. Farmers and other workers often lived outside the city, in the surrounding lowlands. If the city came under attack, people from the lowlands could seek shelter inside the city walls.

Rulers in the Aegean region fortified their cities to protect themselves against foreign invaders. But the city walls also often kept out close neighbors. Great cities such as Argos, Corinth, and Mycenae cooperated with one another. They traded goods, guaranteed travelers safe passage through their lands, and exchanged artists and builders. But they were not above picking fights and raiding one another's cities.

A NEW LIFE

Schliemann must wait out the autumn and winter before beginning his excavations. He travels to Paris, France, to finish writing his book *Ithaka* (about the Greek city of Ithaca). But Troy is still very much on his mind. In December 1868, he writes to Calvert from Paris. To prepare for the excavation, he sends Calvert a long list of questions. Schliemann asks Calvert everything from whether he needs to bring his own pillows to where he should hire workers. He also wants to know how much the whole project will cost. Calvert answers all Schliemann's questions.

Schliemann also uses the winter to make some great changes in his life. In January 1869, Schliemann returns to Russia to try to make peace with Ekaterina. He misses his children very much. But Ekaterina does not miss Schliemann and does not want him to move back.

Schliemann's unhappiness is somewhat relieved in February. After the publication of *Ithaka*, the University of Rostock (in Germany) grants him a doctor of philosophy degree. He is very pleased and insists that he be called Dr. Schliemann from then on.

Schliemann finally decides it is time to end his marriage. He hears that it is easier to get a divorce in certain parts of the United States than in Europe. So in March 1869, he sails for New York. He applies for citizenship after getting an American friend to lie for him. The friend tells the U.S. government that Schliemann has lived in the country for a long time. He gets his citizenship and moves to Indianapolis, Indiana, to begin divorce proceedings.

Even before his divorce is granted, Schliemann begins looking for a new wife. He decides he wants a Greek wife who shares his interest in Homer and ancient history. And he wants a young wife who will look up to him. He writes to a friend in Greece, a priest named Theokletos Vimpos. Vimpos mails Schliemann a photo of his cousin's beautiful daughter, Sophia Engastromenos. Sophia is thirty years younger than Schliemann. But the Engastromenos family is happy to marry their daughter to such a wealthy man.

In July he finally receives his divorce. By then it is too far into the hot summer to return to Hissarlik. Schliemann writes to Calvert that they will have to wait until spring 1870. Instead, Schliemann travels to Athens, Greece, to meet Sophia. They marry on September 23, 1869.

Sophia was seventeen years old when she married Schliemann.

CHAPTER two

DIGGING FOR TROY

Schliemann and Sophia travel to Paris after their wedding. Schliemann immediately begins Sophia's education in ancient history and languages. He wants her to be prepared for their adventures together as archaeologists.

Sophia, however, grows homesick. She tires of the endless reading and daily lessons. Soon she is so unhappy that she cannot stop herself from crying. Her new husband is sorry he has pushed her too hard. In January 1870, they return to Athens. While Sophia rests with her family, Schliemann returns to his plans for Troy.

IN HOT WATER

In February, Schliemann writes to Calvert asking him to get official permission to excavate. Even though Calvert owns part of the hill, Schliemann still must ask the Turkish government for permission to dig for ruins. The government is entitled to part of whatever antiquities he finds. While he waits for the *firman*, or permit, Schliemann cannot rest. He takes a sailing trip around the Aegean Sea. Then he and Sophia visit more historic Greek sites—Delphi, Marathon, and Eleusis.

By April, Schliemann still has not heard back from Calvert. He is anxious to begin the excavation during the cooler spring weather, before

Before excavation, the hill of Hissarlik *(center)* looked like many of the surrounding hills.

the heat of summer begins. Schliemann decides to go to Hissarlik and begin the dig without government permission. He also decides that Calvert's eastern part of the hill is not the best place to start. He begins to dig in the northwestern part—on land owned by local Turkish farmers. Schliemann ignores the farmers' complaints and demands for money. He also ignores warnings from Calvert to wait for the firman.

He first digs up potsherds, bronze nails, stone lance (a long, thin spear) points, and Roman silver coins. Not very exciting finds, Schliemann thinks. But then he finds a vase made to hold human ashes and a terra-cotta (a type of ceramic) statue of a woman's head and shoulders. These are older and more unusual. Schliemann links these artifacts to Homer's Troy. He then hits upon the ruins of some walls. At once, Schliemann writes to scholars in Paris and to a German newspaper. He announces that he has found the walls of Priam's palace.

This is exciting news. Word travels fast through Europe that Schliemann has found evidence of Troy. Unfortunately for Schliemann, word also travels to Constantinople (modern-day Istanbul), the Turkish capital. Along with the farmers' complaints, news of Schliemann's finds gets the attention of the Turkish government. Schliemann must stop all excavations.

Schliemann's illegal digging threatens the whole project. There is a chance that the Turkish government will never grant him a firman. "I cannot conceal how injudicious [unwise] I think it is of you to have made a boast of what you did," Calvert writes Schliemann. The two men have to decide when and how to reapply for the firman. Calvert recommends that they let some time pass, until Turkish government officials are in a better mood.

After a few weeks, Schliemann approaches Turkish officials again. He tries to explain that he did not ask for the farmers' permission because he knew they would say no. He also writes letters of apology to the Turkish government. He asks powerful friends to plead on his behalf.

While he waits for permission to return to Hissarlik, Sophia gives birth to a daughter on May 18, 1871. They name her Andromache, after the wife of the Trojan hero Hector. To house his new family, Schliemann asks Ziller to design a mansion in Athens.

On August 12, Schliemann receives news that he will be given a firman to continue work at Hissarlik. The permit states that Schliemann must turn over one-half of all that he finds to the Turkish government. He must leave ruins in the condition he finds them, and he must pay the entire cost of the excavation. And because the government does not trust Schliemann, they add another condition. A government supervisor will be sent to Hissarlik to watch over the project. Schliemann will have to pay the supervisor's salary.

WINTER 1871

As soon as he receives the firman on October 11, Schliemann begins the dig. Workers have only a few weeks before winter arrives in the Troad. Schliemann still believes that Priam's city rests at the bottom of the hill, 50 feet (15 m) below the surface. His plan to reach those ruins is simple: he will dig a 30-foot (9 m) trench straight down and remove all the rubble that stands in the way. He does not care about the Roman or later Greek cities built on the site. He only cares about finding the Troy described in *The Iliad*.

After just a couple of days, Schliemann sees he does not have enough workers. He increases his staff from eight to eighty. But they have only a few wheelbarrows and four ox-drawn carts. Workers cannot remove dirt and debris fast enough to keep up with the trench digging. To add to the problems, heavy autumn rains begin. When the rains prevent excavation, Schliemann retreats to the small house he has built at Hissarlik. He adds to his diary, works on his notebooks, and writes letters to friends and colleagues.

Stratigraphical Analysis

In the late 1800s, archaeology was still a fairly new science. Archaeologists were not yet using many of the excavation and identification methods modern archaeologists use. But they had begun to use a method called stratigraphical analysis. As human objects, garbage, building ruins, and dirt pile up over the centuries, they form layers, or strata. Archaeologists carefully examine all the layers in relation to each other. The method gives archaeologists an overall picture of an excavation site's history.

Troy was an almost perfect site for stratigraphical analysis. Each new version of the city—there were nine Troys altogether—sat on top of an old version. But as an amateur, Schliemann did not understand stratigraphical analysis when he began digging. As a result, he mixed objects from different periods together. He almost destroyed a clear record of Troy's history for future archaeologists.

Whenever the weather clears, workers carry on digging. But Schliemann's lack of archaeological training causes confusion. When he finds a layer filled with primitive tools, he believes he has reached the Stone Age of the site. That would mean that there was no Bronze Age city here. Distressed, he writes to Calvert. Calvert assures him that he could not have reached the Stone Age so soon. He encourages Schliemann to keep digging.

Soon, Schliemann begins to find ancient pottery and tools that seem to belong to the more advanced Bronze Age. "Since the sixth of this month [November]," he writes in his diary, "there have appeared not only many nails, but also knives, lances, and battle-axes of copper of such elegant workmanship that they can only have been made by a civilized people."

The damp weather and cold winds are making the workers sick. Toward the end of November 1871, the excavation stops for the season. Schliemann is disappointed that he has not yet made a grand discovery. But he is hopeful that he is on the right track.

SPRING AND SUMMER 1872

To prepare for the next dig, Schliemann spends the next few months studying archaeology. He consults books to help him understand the objects he has found. He visits museums and talks to archaeologists about other prehistoric sites in Europe. By early April 1872, he is anxious to get back to work on his dig.

Schliemann has learned from some of the mistakes made last winter. This time he brings many more wheelbarrows and better pickaxes and shovels. He hires a French railroad engineer, Adolphe Laurent, to make maps of the site. And he learns from Frank Calvert and Emile Burnouf, a French archaeologist in Greece, the need to dig more carefully. They urge Schliemann to record exactly where he finds objects. They tell him he should remove the objects carefully, label them, and pack them for storing.

Sophia joins her husband on this dig. She oversees her own excavation area, along with three other work supervisors. Each day, 150 workers remove loads of dirt and rubble. Workers in the trenches are in danger from falling rocks and collapsing walls. They also often run into nests of poisonous snakes the locals call *antelion*. *Antelion* is Greek for "sunset," which locals say is how long someone will survive when bitten by one of the snakes.

Schliemann worries about his workers' health and safety. But he also complains about some of their habits. He is particularly annoyed by the Greeks' love of festivals. Each time there is a religious festival in one of the villages, the laborers refuse to do any work.

Athena's Birds

The Hissarlik site was home to many owls. Schliemann hated their constant screeching. According to Greek myth, owls are sacred to the goddess Athena. But that did not stop Schliemann from ordering workers to shoot the birds on sight.

Archaeologists believe that this owl vase from Troy was made as early as 3000 B.C.

THE SUN METOPE

Schliemann is thrilled at what he finds that spring and early summer. He finds a two-handled cup similar to a cup Homer describes in *The Iliad*. He finds several vases and cups decorated with what looks like an owl's face. Since owls are the goddess Athena's sacred bird, Schliemann links the cups to Athena's temple at Troy. He is convinced he is nearing Troy.

One day a worker discovers another artifact that could be from the temple to Athena. Digging on the eastern side of the hill, the worker finds a metope. A metope is a panel that decorates the top part of the temple, just under the roof. The metope has a sculpture carved in relief—standing out from the surface. Schliemann cleans the sculpture. He is amazed at its detail. It shows the Greek sun god, Helios, clothed in swirling garments. His head is surrounded by a sunburst. He is riding in a chariot drawn by four rearing horses. "Helios here, so to speak, bursts forth from the light of day," Schliemann writes in his notebook, "and sheds the light of his glory overall."

The metope is found on the part of the hill owned by Calvert. Schliemann has agreed to pay Calvert a share of anything found on his land. He writes Calvert that he has found a beautiful piece of temple art. But Schliemann

This sculpture of Helios, the Greek sun god, once crowned a temple dedicated to Athena. Schliemann believed a Trojan temple to Athena lay under or near the Greek temple.

knows that Calvert is still struggling with family money problems. Schliemann drives a hard bargain. He offers Calvert only a small sum for his share of the metope. Finally tired of arguing with Schliemann, Calvert accepts.

Schliemann decides not to notify the Turkish government about the metope. Instead, he smuggles the panel onto a Greek fishing boat bound for Athens.

THE GREAT TOWER

In August, Schliemann and his workers find an ancient wall. It seems to be older than other walls they have found. Schliemann announces that the wall is part of a tower. He says of the find:

> I believe that the Tower once stood on the western edge of the acropolis. [I]ts top would have commanded, not only a view of the whole Plain of Troy, but of the sea with the islands of Tenedos, Imbros, and Samothrace. There is not a more sublime situation in the area of Troy than this, and I therefore presume that this is the "Great Tower of Ilium."

He writes to German and British newspapers that Homer's Troy has been found. "Everyone must admit," he claims, "that I have solved a great historical puzzle." Schliemann now feels free to rename the excavation site. He begins dating his letters and diary entries from "Troy."

But Schliemann wonders at the size of the hill. At most, it measures 600 by 450 feet (183 by 137 m). Those measurements do not match Homer's description of the city. But instead of questioning Homer, Schliemann thinks that the hill contained only part of Priam's fortress. "The Pergamus of Priam . . . must necessarily have extended a good way further south, beyond the high plateau."

Schliemann is more confident than ever about his discoveries. But work on the site ends soon after he finds the tower wall. In the heat of mid-August, some workers become ill with malaria. Sophia and Schliemann return to Athens.

Schliemann uncovered the walls that protected Troy at different times. In this picture, taken from a tower wall, Schliemann identified walls from the Late Bronze Age *(left)*, Greek *(right)*, and Roman *(center)* cities on the hill of Hissarlik.

CHAPTER three

THE TREASURE
OF PRIAM

In January 1873, Schliemann asks the Greek government to allow him to excavate at two ancient Greek cities—Olympia and Mycenae. In exchange, Schliemann promises, he will leave everything he finds to the Greek nation after he dies. The government reminds Schliemann that antiquities found in Greece already belong to the Greek nation. They refuse him permission. Instead, they give a German archaeological team permission to work at Olympia.

Schliemann is insulted by the government's response. But he doesn't spend much time arguing over it. He is anxious to begin working again. By the end of the month, Schliemann and Sophia are back at Troy. It is freezing cold. At night the Schliemanns and their overseer, Photidas, huddle in the wooden house at the excavation site. The winds rush through gaps between the wallboards, and it is hard to keep lamps lit. As they sleep, the temperature in the house falls below 23°F (−5°C).

THE SECOND CITY

Excavation work begins slowly in February, under the watchful eye of a Turkish official, Amin Effendi. Real progress, Schliemann reports, is held up by "Greek church festivals, thunderstorms, and . . . the excessive cold." But by March, 160 workers are on-site.

Workers begin to uncover "many large and beautifully sculpted blocks of marble." Schliemann thinks they may belong to a temple built during the time of Lysimachus (CA. 361–281 B.C.). Lysimachus was a general in the army of Alexander the Great (356–323 B.C.). Alexander was fascinated by Homer and the Trojan War. After Alexander's death, Lysimachus vowed to restore Priam's once-great city in honor of Alexander. Lysimachus called the city Ilion.

On the other hand though, Schliemann thinks, the marble blocks may belong to a Roman temple. Either way, he decides, they "are of no further value to archaeology." Nothing but evidence of Homer's Troy interests Schliemann.

As workers dig deeper, Schliemann begins to realize that he was wrong to think that Troy lay at the very bottom of Hissarlik's hill. The bottom-most layer of the dig is too primitive to have been the legendary Troy. The layer second to the bottom is more likely Priam's city.

THE ASHES OF DESTRUCTION

At this level, Schliemann finds the walls to a fortress. Inside the fortress, workers uncover the walls of houses. Schliemann finds evidence that this version of the city suffered a serious fire—as Priam's Troy had at the end of the war. "Everywhere," he writes, "I find the ashes of destruction." Schliemann also finds a confusing mix of small items—Roman coins, stone tools, and more owl-faced vases.

On April 5, 1873, workers discover a large house directly beneath the ruins of a Greek temple of Athena. Calvert had discovered these temple ruins before he ran out of money. The workers also uncover a broad street. Schliemann thinks it must be the city's "Main Street." If so, it would lead to the Scaean Gate, the major entrance through Troy's walls. Schliemann continues to excavate the street, following its path out toward the edge

Workers use pickaxes to reveal the remains of houses beneath the temple of Athena. Others wait with wheelbarrows to carry away debris. This illustration appeared in one of Schliemann's books in 1881.

of the fortress. There, on May 10, workers hit upon the ruined walls of two buildings. Schliemann judges that one must be the Scaean Gate and the other the palace of Priam.

A MASS OF GOLD

Early one morning in late May, Schliemann makes another discovery. Digging in a wall near what he calls the palace of Priam, he finds a copper item lodged in the dirt. Behind it, he sees the gleam of gold. Before going any further, Schliemann dismisses all his workers. "To withdraw the treasure from the greed of my workmen, and to save it for archaeology, . . . I immediately had 'païdos' [a rest break] called."

Only a trusted Greek assistant, Nicholas Yannakis, remains behind. Schliemann and Yannakis use knives to dig around the copper item. It turns out be a small oval shield about 20 inches (50 centimeters) long. Next, they remove a copper pot, a copper plate, a copper vase, and a silver

Schliemann's Treasure of Priam included these three golden vessels.

vase. "Thereupon followed a globular [rounded] bottle of the purest gold. . . . Then came a cup, likewise of the purest gold. Next came another cup of the purest gold . . . in the form of a ship with two handles. . . ."

The treasure keeps coming. In addition to more gold, copper, and silver cups and plates, the men find silver vases filled with gold jewelry. The jewelry is a "mass of several thousand gold rings and decorative pieces, with gold bracelets, a gold headband, four beautiful earrings, and two splendid gold diadems [a type of crown]." The most elaborate diadem is made of more than "16,000 tiny pieces of gold threaded on gold wire."

HIDING THE TREASURE

Schliemann and Yannakis cover the treasure with cloth and carry it up to Schliemann's house. But a worker spots them with the bundle and reports it to Amin Effendi. Effendi appears at Schliemann's door and demands that he be allowed to search the house. Schliemann refuses and tells Effendi to leave. Schliemann has put off the official for a while. But he knows that the man will come back with Turkish authorities.

Late that afternoon, Schliemann writes a desperate letter to Frederick Calvert, Frank Calvert's brother. "I am closely watched," he writes, "and expect that the Turkish watchman who is angry with me, I do not know for what reason, will search my house tomorrow." Frederick owns a farm not far from Hissarlik, and Schliemann wants to move the treasure there. He begs Frederick Calvert to accept six baskets and one bag filled with jewelry and precious objects. "Kindly lock them up," he asks, "and not allow by any means the Turks to touch them."

Schliemann sends Yannakis off to the Calvert farm with the treasure. Yannakis and another Greek worker, Demetriou, return to the farm a week later. They repack the treasure in crates and load it onto a boat to Athens.

LEAVING TROY

Back at Troy, Schliemann tears down his wooden house. He is leaving Troy, he believes, forever. He knows he has angered the Turkish government again. But he is not troubled by what he has done. He believes the treasure belongs to him, and he will give it to Greece. The treasures of Troy, in Schliemann's mind, do not belong to the Turkish people. Troy is a part of Greek (and so, European) history, not Turkish history. And like other archaeologists of his day, Schliemann believes that certain countries cannot be trusted to take care of the world's archaeological treasures.

Schliemann's excavations cut away the entire top of the hill of Hissarlik. This engraving shows the hill as it appeared at the end of the 1873 excavations.

Caught in a Lie?

When exactly did Schliemann find the Treasure of Priam? Scholars have trouble pinpointing the exact day. In Schliemann's published version of events, he writes about the treasure in his diary from Troy on June 17, 1873. He says Sophia was with him and helped carry the treasure out. But personal letters show that Sophia was in Athens on June 17.

Some scholars explain this gap by suggesting Schliemann wanted to include Sophia in his amazing discovery. But the explanation is not that simple. Evidence exists that Schliemann and Sophia were both back in Athens on June 17. Further, an actual copy of Schliemann's diary page shows that he scratched out information. He changed the diary entry date from May 31 to June 17 and changed the place from Athens to Troy.

Critics think Schliemann was trying to cover up the fact that he did not find the Treasure of Priam all in one place. He gathered up gold objects, they say, found in several places at Troy at different times. Then he put them together and pretended to make one dramatic discovery. Once safely in Athens with the gold, Schliemann reconstructed the discovery in his diary.

His biggest critics suggest that Schliemann never "found" most of the Treasure of Priam at all. They claim he had the famous headpiece and other gold items made by Turkish jewelers.

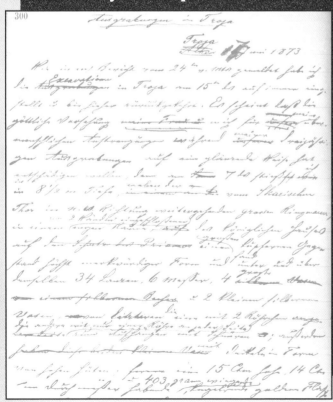

This page from Schliemann's journal documents the discovery of Priam's treasure. The date at the top right has been changed.

Sophia Schliemann wears the Jewels of Helen in this illustration, which was copied from a photograph. Gold wires held the necklaces and diadem together for thousands of years, enabling the archaeologist to keep the pieces close to their original appearance.

Once in Athens, Schliemann announces the discovery of the Treasure of Priam to the world. He calls the most elaborate diadem the Jewels of Helen. He has Sophia photographed wearing the crown with its delicate pendants of gold beads. Newspaper readers devour descriptions of the jewelry. Scholars debate Schliemann's interpretations of his find. Gold hunters descend on Hissarlik.

In the midst of all this publicity, Schliemann packs up Priam's treasure in bundles. He sends a bundle to each of several of Sophia's relatives for safekeeping. He has no intention of turning the treasure over to the Greek government—not yet anyway.

The giant stone blocks of the Cyclopean walls frame the Lion Gate of Mycenae. The Lion Gate was discovered by Kyriakos Pittakis, a Greek archaeologist, in 1841.

CHAPTER four
MYCENAE

To Schliemann, the Treasure of Priam proves that Troy had once been a wealthy city, just as Homer claimed. The position of the treasure, Schliemann believes, showed that servants were trying to carry the treasure out of the palace during some catastrophe. They had to drop the treasure when they were stopped by a terrible fire—like the one that destroyed Priam's Troy.

Schliemann has to admit that Troy is not all that he had dreamed it to be. He has not found an enormous palace filled with storerooms of gold. But he feels that the discoveries of 1873 have proved that legendary Troy really existed.

Later in the summer of 1873, Schliemann begins work on his next book, *Troy and Its Remains*. He also again asks the Greek government for permission to excavate Mycenae. If Troy is the end point of the Trojan War, Mycenae is its beginning. It is from Mycenae that Agamemnon and Menelaus raise the Achaean army.

AGAMEMNON'S CITY

Mycenae was already in ruins when the Greek geographer Pausanias visited it in A.D. 170. Pausanias could still see the city's Cyclopean walls. Walls and houses are called Cyclopean when they are constructed of enormous stone blocks. The blocks are so large that ancient legends claimed they were lifted into place by the Cyclopes, giants of Greek myth. Pausanias also described the royal tombs of Agamemnon and his father, Atreus.

Those tombs, Pausanias wrote, were inside the city's citadel, or fortress. The few archaeologists who visited Mycenae thought that Pausanias simply meant the tombs were within the city's outer walls. They did not think the tombs were within the citadel. Why would the Mycenaeans waste limited space within the fortress on a cemetery?

But Schliemann takes Pausanias at his word. He wants to dig for the royal tombs inside the citadel. When scholars and the press hear of Schliemann's plans, they make fun of him. A London newspaper, the *Times,* writes an editorial slyly referring to rumors that the Treasure of Priam was a fake. The editorial claims there's only one way Schliemann will find Mycenae's royal tombs inside the citadel—if he puts them there and then pretends to discover them.

IN TROUBLE AGAIN

Schliemann ignores the critics and waits for his government permit. But by February 1874, he cannot wait any longer. He is too restless at home in Athens. He and Sophia leave for Mycenae. Schliemann says that he is only going to look over the site. But he plans to start digging—with or without permission.

When Schliemann arrives at Mycenae, he tells local authorities that he has government permission to dig. The Schliemanns are joined at Mycenae by Emile Burnouf, the French scholar. The Schliemanns hire more than twenty workers to dig thirty-four small trenches within the citadel. The team digs for five days, finding many small terra-cotta statues and some ancient pottery. Within the citadel, the team also finds some undecorated stelae—stone slabs usually used to mark graves.

Before the excavations go any further, the local police chief realizes Schliemann has lied about the permit. The chief stops the dig. In March 1874, Schliemann gets news that the Greek government will give him the permit. But before Schliemann can start work again, he learns that the Turkish government is suing him in a Greek court. The Turks want Schliemann to pay for having illegally removed antiquities from Troy. Schliemann will have to return to Athens for the trial.

The case continues through July. When the court breaks for a summer recess, Schliemann makes plans to travel to central Greece and the Peloponnese (the southern part of mainland Greece). Just as he is about to leave, he hears that the Greek government is withdrawing its permission. He cannot return to Mycenae.

Finally, in April 1875, the Turkish trial ends. Schliemann is ordered to pay the Turkish government a large fine for having removed the Treasure of Priam. The money will be given to the Turkish Imperial Museum. Schliemann pays the Turks five times what he is ordered to pay. He also sends the museum a shipment of nonprecious antiquities found at Troy. Schliemann is relieved the trial is over—and relieved that the real treasures of Troy belong to him alone.

A CELEBRITY IN EUROPE

Schliemann decides to leave Athens. Throughout the summer of 1875, he travels in Europe. He visits old friends and contacts in the archaeological world. In Paris he lectures at the Société Géographique (Geographical Society) on his Troy discoveries. In June he appears before the Society of Antiquaries of London. His lecture on Troy is a huge success, drawing a large and enthusiastic audience. Schliemann becomes a celebrity in London.

Schliemann also travels to the Netherlands, Sweden, Denmark, and Poland. At each stop, he visits local museums and universities and talks to archaeologists. In Germany Schliemann meets Rudolf Virchow, a famous professor, a medical doctor, and a scholar of prehistory. Virchow and Schliemann become friends.

Schliemann gives a speech about his work at Mycenae to members of the Society of Antiquaries of London.

In the autumn, Schliemann goes to Italy. He is looking for a new site to excavate. But he cannot find anything that interests him. In December he decides to return to Troy.

BACK TO DIGGING

Schliemann leaves Italy for Constantinople in January 1876. He tries to get a new firman from the Turkish government. After four months of negotiations, Schliemann gets his permit and leaves at once for Troy. But excavations do not go well. Frank Calvert has had enough of Schliemann and will not give him any more help. The local Turkish authorities cause problems for him. Schliemann finally loses patience. He quits Troy and returns to Greece.

In August 1876, Schliemann hears good news from the Greek government. They will allow him to renew excavations at Mycenae. According to the permit, the Greek Archaeological Society will oversee this operation. Schliemann is very irritated. He does not want to be watched over by any archaeological society.

The society sends Panagiotis Stamatakis to Mycenae as the overseer. Stamatakis is a talented young archaeologist. But Schliemann looks upon him as a government clerk. From the start, he makes life miserable for Stamatakis. Stamatakis writes to the Athens government, "He treats me as if I was a barbarian. . . . If the ministry is not satisfied with me, I beg that I be recalled; I remain here at the expense of my health."

AROUND THE LION GATE

Despite this conflict, Schliemann starts work at the Mycenae acropolis on August 7, 1876. He has sixty-three workers divided into three groups working inside and outside the Cyclopean walls. Twelve workers dig around the city's famous Lion Gate. They are trying "to open the passage into the acropolis." Forty-three workers begin digging a trench about 40 feet (12 m) away from the gate. The remaining eight workers begin a trench on the south side of a large structure that is almost completely buried. The structure is a tholos (*plural* tholoi), a beehive-shaped building. This tholos has been known since Pausanias's day as the Treasury of Atreus.

The Tholoi

Pausanias thought the tholoi at Mycenae were storehouses for the city's gold and treasures. He called the large tholos outside the Lion Gate the Treasury of Atreus. But that idea was challenged by Carl Schuchhardt (1859–1943), a German university professor. Schuchhardt did not believe that the Mycenaeans would store their treasures outside the city walls, where they would be unprotected. Schuchhardt thought the tholoi were tombs. He has since been proved correct. Other tholoi have been found near Mycenae containing funeral items and human remains.

Excavations continue through August. Schliemann grows nervous about the workers digging around the Lion Gate and the surrounding Cyclopean walls. The Cyclopean walls are 13 to 35 feet (4 to 11 m) high and more than 16 feet (5 m) thick. In some places, the enormous blocks of stone have tumbled down. The area does not seem safe. The archaeological society promises to send an engineer to Mycenae to secure the wall and the gate's stone lions.

THE ROYAL GRAVES

While he waits for the engineer to arrive, Schliemann stops work on that area. He begins another large trench in which he finds many small vases and statues. In early September, he finds two stelae decorated with relief carvings.

Schliemann digs down 27 feet (8 m). He has reached the bedrock—the stone layer beneath all the soil. Schliemann thinks they have nothing more to find in this area. But in early December, he discovers a shaft grave, a type of tomb dug into the natural rock.

Schliemann and Sophia kneel on the ground around the opening to the tomb. Sophia uses a penknife to begin removing objects. Piece after piece, they find gold diadems, golden drinking cups, golden belts, rings, breastplates, and gemstones. The gold alone weighs 33 pounds (15 kilograms). They also find ceramics, bronze and copper tools, daggers

A guide stands at the entrance to the circle of royal graves in 1906. Mycenae became a popular tourist destination after Schliemann's discoveries.

(knives) inlaid with gold, silver, and a blue stone called lapis lazuli. There are gold and ivory boxes, silver drinking cups, and bowls carved of rock crystal.

In all, the Schliemanns discover five grave shafts inside the citadel. Beneath all the gold and treasure, they discover the remains of nineteen men and women and two infants. The amount of treasure buried with these bodies suggests that the people were royalty. Schliemann believes that the bodies belong to Agamemnon and the people who returned to Mycenae with him after the Trojan War.

Agamemnon's Death

Agamemnon survived the Trojan War, but he did not live long afterward. In his ten-year absence, Agamemnon's wife, Clytemnestra, had fallen in love with another man, Aegisthus. When Agamemnon returned to Mycenae, Clytemnestra and Aegisthus murdered him and took his throne. Eight years later, Agamemnon and Clytemnestra's children Orestes and Electra avenged their father's death by killing their mother. The murder and the tragic revenge are part of the curse that the ancient Greeks believed hung over the House of Atreus. The story of Agamemnon's death is retold in some of ancient Greece's most famous literature. These works include *The Odyssey* (by Homer) and the famous Greek plays *The Oresteia* (by Aeschylus) and *Electra* (by Sophocles).

THE DEATH MASK OF AGAMEMNON

Gold masks had been placed over the faces of four of the men at the time of burial. One of the masks has preserved the face underneath. "Both eyes perfectly visible," Schliemann notes, "also the mouth, which . . . showed thirty-two beautiful teeth."

One of the gold masks is crushed. Another shows a middle-aged, round-faced man. The mask over the preserved face is that of an older man—"a man of power and determination." It is a thin face, with a long, straight nose and large eyes. Schliemann believes that he has found the gold death mask of the leader of the Achaeans. He telegraphs the Greek minister of education that he has seen the face of Agamemnon.

The Death Mask of Agamemnon

AN AMAZING FIND

Five bodies are too badly decomposed to be saved. Some of the remains fall apart as soon as the fresh air hits them. But many of the bones and skulls of the other bodies have been preserved in their graves. Workers cut into rock all the way around some of the bodies. The workers lift the entire slab out of the grave. The remains are moved to a nearby village, Charvati. There they are packed up and sent to the National Museum in Athens.

As usual, Schliemann immediately publicizes his discovery. He writes to several European newspapers in detail. Word also spreads locally. People are amazed that twenty-one Bronze Age human bodies and fabulous gold treasure have been found at the long-ignored site. "News . . . spread like wildfire through the Argolid [the region around Mycenae]," Schliemann notes in his diary, "and people came by the thousands." Schliemann must post soldiers to guard the site. He wants to keep local people from making their own excavations at night.

Was Schliemann Right?

According to Homer, the dead bodies of Bronze Age people were cremated (burned) on funeral pyres (fires). The bodies of several heroes in *The Iliad* were treated this way. Schliemann insisted he saw evidence of cremation in the Mycenaean shaft graves. But if that were true, not as much would remain of the bodies. More likely, Schliemann saw traces of small fires lit at the time of the burials. Schliemann also believed that all people in the shaft graves were buried at the same time. That would match the legends that Agamemnon and his friends were murdered together. But it was common for shaft graves to be reused. Modern archaeologists believe that the first people buried in the shaft graves actually lived one thousand years before the Trojan War.

AFTERMATH

To scholars and archaeologists, the artifacts from Mycenae are more than just fabulous treasure. They are clues about life in the ancient kingdom. The alabaster (a soft stone) vessels are probably from Egypt. The carved ivory and amber jewelry are from the Baltic region of eastern Europe. Many of the pots and cups are similar to ceramics found throughout the Mediterranean region. These clues all suggest regular trade between Mycenae and other lands. That level of trade would have required diplomacy and cooperation. The clues also suggest some cultural exchange—an interest in other countries' art and architecture.

"By themselves alone these treasures are enough to fill a great museum, which will be the world's most wonderful and which for centuries to come will draw thousands of foreigners from all countries to Greece."

—Heinrich Schliemann, writing to King George I of Greece,
after discovering royal tombs at Mycenae, 1876

In 1876 these are new ideas. The Mycenaean treasures are a glimpse into Greece's unknown past. They reveal a culture much more sophisticated than scholars had imagined. Along with the finds at Troy, the treasures seemed to suggest that the Bronze Age was a golden time before the dark age, just as Homer's Greeks believed.

Different layers of construction can be seen in the exposed walls at Troy. Schliemann destroyed evidence of earlier settlements in his pursuit of one particular layer.

CHAPTER five

RETURN TO TROY

Mycenae proves to be an enormous success for Schliemann. Scholars are fascinated by the royal graves. Tourists from all over the world fill Greece's hotels, waiting for a glimpse of the gold masks and other treasures.

Schliemann's status as an archaeologist grows. In 1877 the German Anthropological Society names him an honorary member. Great Britain's Royal Archaeological Society gives him a medal. At the medal ceremony in London, he and Sophia give speeches to great applause.

Schliemann enjoys his fame very much. But not everything is going well. Schliemann begins to complain of headaches and earaches. He admits that they have been bothering him for a while. He also admits that he is losing his hearing. Sophia urges him to see a doctor. But the fifty-five-year-old Schliemann believes that good food and exercise will keep him healthy. He does not realize that his favorite exercise—swimming in the sea—may be at the root of his ear problems. The salt water seeping into his ears is causing one ear infection after another.

SCHLIEMANNOPOLIS

Schliemann has had a permit for another excavation at Troy since January 1876. But he does not return to Troy for two years. He travels again and works on his book, *Mycenae*. He also goes back to Ithaca. He wants to find some sites associated with the Greek hero Odysseus. Homer tells the story of Odysseus's long journey home to Ithaca after the Trojan War in *The Odyssey*. Schliemann finds 190 houses with Cyclopean walls at Ithaca, along with some ancient pottery shards. But he does not find much that he can match to Homer's tale.

In September 1878, Schliemann returns to Troy. He hires a large number of workers and rents many horse carts. On the northwest slope of Hissarlik, he begins building a nine-room barracks for himself and his family, his overseers, the servants, and any visitors to the site. Separate from the barracks, he builds a wood house for the security guards he calls gendarmes. He also builds a storehouse and dining hall, a stone kitchen, a shed for tools and machines, and a stable for the horses. Visitors jokingly call the collection of buildings Schliemannopolis.

For two months, he and his workers excavate the site for fourteen hours a day. They are trying to clear all the rubble from the building Schliemann calls Priam's Palace. Schliemann also wants to work outward

This photograph shows "Schliemannopolis" around 1878.

from the Scaean Gate, tracing as much of the city wall as he can. During these excavations, Schliemann finds bronze weapons and more terra-cotta jars filled with gold and silver jewelry. None of it is as spectacular as the Treasure of Priam. But it is more evidence of the city's wealth. This time Schliemann turns two-thirds of his finds over to Turkey's Imperial Museum.

LEARNED FRIENDS

Winter weather ends the dig in November. Schliemann goes home to Athens but returns as soon as possible, in late February 1879. The north wind, Schliemann recalled later, was "so icy cold that it was impossible to read or write in my wooden barracks." To keep from catching a cold, Schliemann takes a daily swim in the sea, riding his horse to the shore before dawn.

For this season, he hires 150 workers and ten gendarmes. On March 1, excavations begin. Schliemann repairs his friendship with Frank Calvert, and Calvert joins the work. Calvert begins exploring the Troad for tumuli—mounds made by humans that mark gravesites. He is looking for signs of human burial. According to Homer, the Trojans cremated their dead. They buried the remains and funeral treasures under tumuli. At other periods, the people who lived in Troy would have buried dead bodies in a necropolis (cemetery) somewhere around Hissarlik.

At the end of March, two more friends join the Troy excavations—Emile Burnouf and Rudolf Virchow. Burnouf plans to make maps of Troy for the publication of *Ilios*—the book Schliemann is preparing about Troy. He will also sketch the artifacts and the landscape of Hissarlik. Virchow wants to look at the geology (the rocks, soil, and other physical features) of the plain of Troy.

Schliemann very much wants to remain in charge of Troy. He calls Burnouf and Virchow—both much more educated than himself—his assistants. Yet he is proud to work alongside them and Calvert. He sees the value of having different types of experts working on an archaeological site.

A Second Agamemnon

Sophia gave birth to a baby boy on March 16, 1878. The Schliemanns named him Agamemnon. Sophia wanted Agamemnon baptized into the Greek Orthodox religion. Schliemann agreed, but only if he were allowed to hold a copy of *The Iliad* over Agamemnon's head during prayers. At the baptism, Schliemann worried that the water in the baptismal font was not a good temperature for the baby's health. In the middle of the ceremony, Schliemann stuck a thermometer in the water. This caused an argument between Schliemann and the priest. Sophia had to calm down the priest and convince her husband to let the ceremony continue.

THE BURNED CITY

In the summer of 1879, Burnouf identifies seven strata at Troy. The strata represent seven cities, each built on top of an earlier destroyed city. The third city from the bottom shows clear signs of having been destroyed by a fire.

Schliemann begins excavating this layer house by house. All that is left of the houses are the foundations. The foundations have no doors, so Schliemann thinks they must have been storage cellars. He seems to be right. Soon workers uncover large jars called *pithoi*. Pithoi were used to store olive oil, grains, and other household goods. Some pithoi were taller than an adult man. They would have been kept in a house's cellar.

Virchow helps confirm this idea. A medical doctor, he has been visiting local homes to help the sick. He recognizes the kind of house Schliemann is finding in this layer. The Trojan houses are almost

When Schliemann uncovered these pithoi, they were intact. Workers broke them open against his wishes, hoping to find treasure.

exactly the same as those still used in the Troad. Virchow confirms that the lower level of the house is indeed a storage cellar. The family lives in the upper story.

AN IMAGINARY CITY?

The 1879 season ends late that summer. Schliemann returns to Athens. The Schliemanns' new home is finished. He and Sophia call the mansion Iliou Melathron—the House of Ilium. They name it after the first wooden house they built at Hissarlik.

That fall Schliemann begins writing *Ilios*. Once again, he says that he has finished his work at Troy. In his notes, he claims that he has reached the "great aim of my life." But as he begins setting down his story of the 1878–1879 excavations, doubts trouble him. He thinks of the treasure he found at Mycenae. If Agamemnon's city and Priam's city existed at the same time, why do they seem so different? And if Troy was so small, why would it have taken the Achaeans ten years to conquer it?

In November, Schliemann writes to Brockhaus, his German publisher, to give the company an update on *Ilios*. In the letter, he voices these doubts. If Troy ever did exist, he writes, then what he has found at Hissarlik is it. But that is a big "if." "Now the only question," he acknowledges, "is whether Troy has only existed in the poet's imagination or in reality."

WHERE WILL THE TREASURES GO?

In his excavation diaries, Schliemann declares that he will never sell his portion of the antiquities he has found. But he is unsure what to do with them. He has strong ties to France, Great Britain (where his antiquities are currently being kept), the United States, Germany, and Greece. To which of those countries should he give his Trojan and Mycenaean treasures? Virchow convinces Schliemann to give the antiquities to his native land, Germany. Sophia is angry that the treasures will not go to Greece. Schliemann is also afraid he has angered allies in Great Britain and the United States. But he goes through with his plans. In the winter of 1880, Schliemann travels to London to supervise the packing of the Troy artifacts. Forty boxes in all are shipped to Berlin.

The Schliemanns have much work ahead of them. They have to unpack and arrange the antiquities in Berlin's new Museum fur Volkerkunde (a museum of ethnic cultures). But as always, Schliemann is restless. Early in 1881, he, Sophia, and friends travel to two ancient Greek cities, Orchomenos and Olympia. A team of German archaeologists is excavating Olympia. Schliemann befriends a member of the team, Dr. Wilhelm Dorpfeld. Dorpfeld is a twenty-seven-year-old German architect. Schliemann is impressed by the younger man's talents.

In the summer of 1881, the Schliemanns finish decorating their house. The mansion stands on University Street (present-day Venizelos Street). The famous ancient Acropolis is visible from its balconies. Twenty-four statues of Greek gods and goddesses stand along the flat roof. Inside, the walls are painted with scenes from Schliemann's life. Views of Indianapolis and New York mix with scenes of the Schliemann children dressed as putti (winged babies). Schliemann has decorated the interior with many works of art and precious objects. But when it comes to the furniture, Schliemann follows the ancient Greek style—very little furniture and none of it covered in fabric. The Schliemanns are proud of their home. Visitors are always welcomed.

"Schliemann is hugely celebrated here [in Germany]. Nevertheless he is and remains half-mad, a man of confused ideas who has no idea of the value of his discoveries."

—Adolf Furtwangler, curator of the Berlin Museum fur Volkerkunde, 1881

THE THIRD SEASON

In March 1882, Schliemann returns to Troy for the third season of excavations. He finds all his equipment in good order, thanks to his Turkish watchman. To fill the kitchen at Schliemannopolis, a British merchant friend sends a shipment of food. The shipment includes cans of "corned

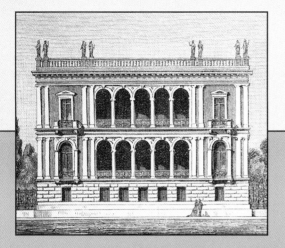

Iliou Melathron, Schliemann's home in Athens

"He built us a veritable [real] palace to live in, but it contained not one stick of comfortable furniture. . . . As a gentle hint, Mother made him a present of an armchair, but he banished it to the garden."

—Andromache Schliemann, recalling the interior of her childhood home, Iliou Melathron

beef, peaches, the best English cheese, and ox-tongues, as well as 240 bottles of the best English ale."

Mid-month, Wilhelm Dorpfeld arrives. Schliemann has convinced the young architect to help him at Troy. Schliemann is beginning to think he has not dug deep enough or wide enough. He wants to pursue the idea that Hissarlik's hill was just the citadel. Only the royal family lived in the citadel, while regular Trojans lived outside the walls. He hopes Dorpfeld's training and talent can "be utilized to restore the reality of Homer."

Schliemann and Dorpfeld begin work on a part of the eastern section of the hill. It is an area that Schliemann has not spent much time exploring. They begin to dig a trench 260 feet (80 m) long and 23 feet (7 m) wide. They are looking for buildings at the early second and first layers.

While Dorpfeld supervises this work, Schliemann begins digging in the plain of Troy. He sinks shafts in the plain. He is looking for the larger city that stood outside the citadel. Schliemann also hopes to find the city's necropolis.

Inside the citadel, Dorpfeld shows Schliemann that the first level of Troy was a small, fortified town. The second level of Troy was a larger city. Dorpfeld and his team find the foundations of two very large buildings in this city. Each building was about 33 feet (10 m) wide and 100 feet (30 m) long. What Schliemann had thought was the burned ruins of the third city are really parts of the second city. The team identifies this city's royal palace, two temples, and several other smaller buildings.

In very little time, Dorpfeld clears up "much of the hopeless jigsaw puzzle of intertwined walls, jumbled blocks of stone, warren [maze] of ditches, and amorphous [shapeless] masses of debris." Other archaeologists begin to call the young architect "Schliemann's greatest discovery."

Like Schliemann, Dorpfeld believes the lower city extended down the east, south, and southwest sides of the hill to the plain. But they find little evidence of houses, workshops, or stables. They find no evidence of a necropolis. The lower city remains a mystery.

Nevertheless, Schliemann announces that the city matches perfectly Homer's description of Troy. Having established this, he says, "My work at Troy is now ended forever, after extending over more than the period of ten years." His final word on Troy—at least for the time being—is published in *Troja* in 1884.

William Dorpfeld poses inside a jar uncovered at Troy.

Thermopylae and Marathon

Marathon and Thermopylae were sites of two of the most famous battles of ancient history. In 490 B.C., Greek armies defended Marathon against invasion by King Darius I of Persia. Ten years later, in 480 B.C., the Spartan king Leonidas and three hundred warriors gathered at Thermopylae. There they fought to the death against the large invading army of the Persian king Xerxes.

SEARCHING FOR HISTORY

Even after claiming his life work is done, Schliemann is looking for new adventures. Soon after writing *Troja*, he explores the ancient sites of Thermopylae and Marathon in central Greece. In 1884 he tries to make plans to excavate at Knossos on the island of Crete. Several years earlier, Minos Kalokairinos, a Cretan merchant, had found the partial ruins of an ancient palace at Knossos. As yet, no one has excavated the site. Schliemann hopes for another amazing discovery at Knossos. But he cannot reach a financial deal with the owner of the land around the ruins.

Schliemann and Sophia turned their attention to Tiryns, the city of the Achaean hero Hercules. Dorpfeld joins them on this trip. The ruins of Tiryns lie 9 miles (14 km) south of Mycenae. Tiryns is very much like Troy and Mycenae. It has Cyclopean walls and a long street leading to its gates.

Schliemann leaves most of the work at Tiryns to Dorpfeld. Dorpfeld's excavation team finds the "outlines of a vast and intricate building complex." One of the buildings is a palace with a large porch and many rooms, including a bathroom with a terra-cotta tub. Clearing out the debris, the team sees that the rooms are full of rich decoration. The walls are covered in alabaster inlaid with blue glass. On the floors are mosaics— pictures made with small, colored stones. Like Troy and Mycenae, Tiryns shows modern archaeologists how advanced Aegean civilizations were.

Working so closely with Schliemann, Dorpfeld notices that the older man seems tired and easily irritated. But Schliemann will not slow down. In early 1886, he travels alone to Central America and the Caribbean region. In 1887 and early 1888, he makes two trips to Egypt. He travels through Europe in the fall of 1888. He returns to Greece in December and spends the next few months traveling around the Aegean.

A CHALLENGE TO TROY

Among Schliemann's German critics is retired army officer Ernst Botticher. Since the publication of *Troja*, Botticher has been writing articles and essays attacking the book. Hissarlik, he claims, is not the ruined Troy of *The Iliad*. It is not the ruins of any city. According to Botticher, Hissarlik is a necropolis left behind by Assyrians or Persians (two groups of people from the ancient Middle East).

Schliemann's friends try to convince him to ignore Botticher. But Botticher's writings are getting a lot of notice among archaeologists. Schliemann fights back by organizing conferences of experts who agree with him. Then, in the fall of 1889, Schliemann invites Botticher to meet him and Dorpfeld at Troy.

Botticher at first refuses the invitation. When he does visit Hissarlik, he leaves unconvinced that it is the legendary Troy. But something good does come

This model shows Troy as it might have appeared in the generation before the events of *The Iliad*.

of Schliemann's argument with Botticher. It draws the interest of more experts. They visit Troy and agree with Schliemann's interpretations. Schliemann decides to start another excavation.

THE GREAT SCHLIEMANN

On March 1, 1890, work resumes at Troy. Dorpfeld discovers another large building. It is a rectangular hall with a central hearth, or fireplace. This suggests that it was a public hall, where a ruler might hold court. Nearby, Dorpfeld finds pottery fragments similar to those found in the Mycenaean graves. Dorpfeld calls this level the sixth city. He feels that this was the Troy of *The Iliad*.

This means that the Treasure of Priam (found in the second city) does not match the dates of the Trojan War. The treasure would be about one thousand years older than Schliemann thought. All the gold he had imagined belonging to Homer's Trojans heroes actually belonged to unnamed, unknown people.

"We could describe Schliemann's excavations on the hill of Hissarlik and consider the results without speaking of Troy or even alluding to it; even then, those discoveries would retain their value; even then, they would have added a whole new chapter to the history of civilization, the history of art."

—Georges Perrot, *Journal des Savants* [Scholars' Journal], 1891

It is a difficult discovery for Schliemann, but he trusts Dorpfeld's expertise. The excavation season ends in August. Schliemann plans to return to Athens and go over all his research. At the same time, Dorpfeld will begin writing his report on his new theory.

But before Schliemann can begin work, he gets another terrible earache. In November he travels to Germany to see Hermann Schwartz, a doctor who specializes in ear problems. Schwartz operates on Schliemann's ear.

Schwartz tells Schliemann not to travel until the surgery has healed. But Schliemann wants to spend Christmas with Sophia and the children. He leaves Germany on December 12. On his way home to Athens, he must stop in Paris because his ear hurts so much. A visit to a French doctor seems to help. Schliemann feels so much better that he decides to take a short trip to Naples, Italy, to see Pompeii again.

But in Naples, Schliemann's ear pains grow much worse. He has to delay his return to Athens. On Christmas Day, Schliemann leaves his hotel without any identification. While hurrying across a city square, the Piazza Carita, he collapses. When passersby come to his rescue, he cannot speak or walk. He is carried into a police station. In his pocket, police officers find a prescription bottle with his doctor's name. The doctor instructs officers to take Schliemann to the Grand Hotel, where he will meet them.

At the Grand Hotel, the Polish novelist Henryk Sienkiewicz is standing in the lobby as the police arrive with an unconscious man. The manager of the hotel asks Sienkiewicz if he knows who the man is. "No," Sienkiewicz says. "That," the hotel manager informs him, "is the great Schliemann." Sienkiewicz watches as the officers carry the frail man, alone and sick in a strange city, up the stairs. Poor "great" Schliemann, he thinks.

The doctor soon arrives, but there is little he can do. Schliemann has suffered a stroke. He dies on December 26, 1890. Dorpfeld and Sophia's oldest brother bring his body back to Athens. At his funeral on January 4, 1891, copies of *The Iliad* and *The Odyssey* are placed in his coffin. King George I of Greece, foreign ambassadors, scholars, and friends attend the services. After the funeral, Schliemann's coffin is placed in a tomb in the First Cemetery of Athens. Designed by Ernst Ziller, the tomb is meant to look like a Greek temple.

In the years after Schliemann's death, excavations uncovered many more ruins on the hill.

EPILOGUE

After Schliemann's death, Dorpfeld carried on excavations at Troy until 1894. In all, he identified nine layers or cities. Those cities were eventually numbered with roman numerals—Troy I through Troy IX. The nine phases showed that humans lived at the site from about 3000 B.C. to about A.D. 600.

Dorpfeld continued to believe that Troy VI—the city that matches some of the pottery found in the royal shaft graves at Mycenae—was Homer's Troy. He believed Troy VI was destroyed by a Greek army about 1250 B.C. "The citadel was completely destroyed by enemy action," he wrote in 1902. "We distinguished traces of a great fire in many places." Further, Dorpfeld found evidence of war—weapons and terra-cotta "bullets" from slingshots that seemed to be Greek-made.

In 1932 American archaeologists from the University of Cincinnati arrived at Troy. Led by Carl Blegen, the team worked at the site for six years. They identified forty-six sublayers of the nine cities. The sublayers represented rebuilding in existing cities, probably after earthquakes or other disasters. Dorpfeld was proven correct that Troy VI is the same age and civilization as the Mycenaean tombs. But Blegen concluded that Troy VIIa was the site of a destructive war and fire.

The Missing Treasure

In the 1940s, the Treasure of Priam was at the center of another plot to smuggle the ancient gold out of a country. World War II (1939-1945) had raged in Europe since 1939. Germany's Nazi government began packing up Berlin's museum artifacts and artwork. If Germany lost and Berlin fell to the Allies, the Nazis did not want their national treasures in enemy hands.

In April 1945, Berlin did fall to the USSR (a union of fifteen republics that included Russia). A group of Russian soldiers found a lone German officer fiercely guarding some wooden packing crates. The Nazi demanded to speak to the soldiers' commanding officer. He begged the officer not to let the soldiers open the crates and loot the contents. The officer was baffled, but he agreed. He had the crates shipped unopened to Moscow, the Russian capital. What became of the Treasure of Priam remained a mystery for more than four decades.

During the Cold War (1945-1991), former allies became enemies. The USSR and the West (the United States, Great Britain, and other non-Communist countries) began a decades-long tension between them. Russia, isolated, kept a mass of secrets in the maze of Moscow's government buildings. One day in 1987, Grigorii Kozlov, a museum curator, was cleaning old papers out of a government office. He ran across a strange document and began reading. Kozlov soon realized that he had found a paper trail to art and artifacts seized during World War II.

In 1994 the Pushkin Museum in Moscow admitted that those seized articles included the Treasure of Priam and many other pieces from the Schliemann Collection. In 1996 the museum exhibited the Trojan treasures for the first time in more than fifty years.

This ritual war hammer is one of the Trojan artifacts exhibited at the Pushkin Museum.

During the twentieth century, archaeologists explored the layers of Troy that had not interested Schliemann. This picture shows Roman temple buildings from New Ilium, the last town to occupy the site.

MODERN EXCAVATIONS

Since 1988 a team of German archaeologists have been working in the Troad. Led by Manfred Korfmann, the team discovered something Schliemann had long sought—evidence of funeral rites. At Besik Tepe, 5 miles (8 km) southwest of Hissarlik, they traced the seashore where it would have been during the Trojan War. Nearby, they found signs of cremation and burial treasure. Some of the treasure was clearly Greek. Some of it even seemed to bear symbols belonging to Mycenaean nobility.

On the hill at Hissarlik, the archaeologists have mapped the walls of Troy VI. About 400 yards (365 m) beyond the city walls, the team found a ditch and a mud-brick defensive wall. This evidence suggested that Troy VI extended beyond the citadel. It covered most of the southern end of the plateau on which Hissarlik sits. The size of this town suggests that about six thousand people lived there. By Bronze Age standards, that would have been a large town. This evidence seems to answer the question of why Troy would have been the scene of a war. The city was large and prosperous enough to attract raiding warriors.

Like Blegen, Korfmann believes that Troy VIIa was destroyed by a war. Research shows that the war probably took place about 1180 B.C. Excavators have found signs of a great fire, some skeletons, and many slingshot bullets.

Other evidence suggests that people from the same ethnic group lived at Hissarlik from the early Bronze Age through the eighth century B.C. The tale of the war that destroyed the city might have been passed on by locals from the time of that Trojan War to Homer's day. If so, Homer would have heard the story from people who knew the area and could have preserved the story's details.

Some archaeologists believe that Hissarlik was abandoned during the region's dark age. In Homer's time, the city stood in ruins. But, Korfmann suggested, the ruins of, "both the citadel and the lower city were still impressive." Homer would have been able to visit those ruins and describe them in his epic. He might have made Troy much larger and grander in his epic poem. But he could have used his knowledge of the general layout of the Hissarlik site and the surrounding landscape. This could explain why *The Iliad* so closely matches the archaeological evidence.

Even if Hissarlik cannot be identified beyond a doubt as Homer's Troy, the site's value is clear. Since Schliemann's day, archaeologists have recognized the importance of the discoveries at Troy. As historian Michael Wood notes, it is "one of the key sites in the Mediterranean world for what it tells us about the continuity and development of human civilization in the Aegean and Asia Minor."

EXCAVATION AT HISSARLIK (TROY)

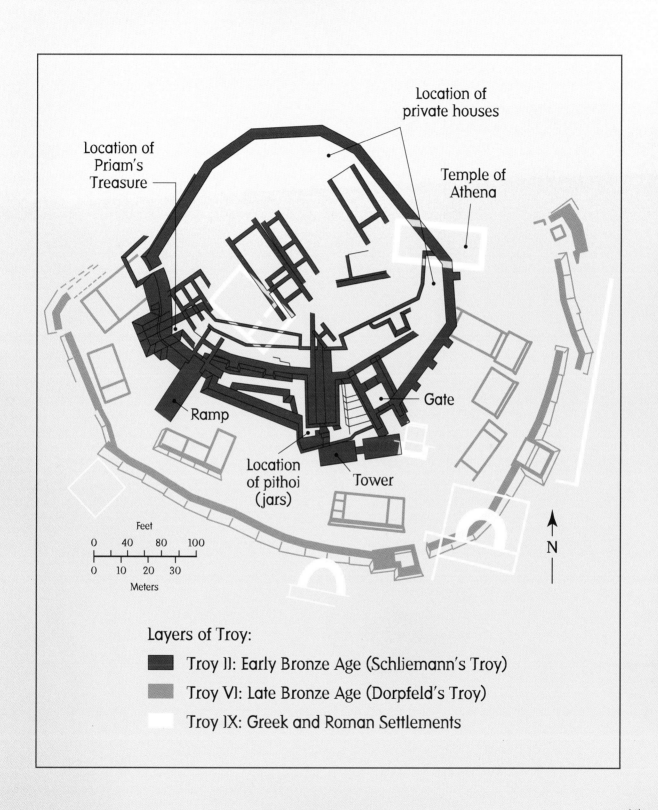

Location of private houses

Location of Priam's Treasure

Temple of Athena

Ramp

Gate

Location of pithoi (jars)

Tower

Feet

| 0 | 40 | 80 | 100 |

| 0 | 10 | 20 | 30 |

Meters

N

Layers of Troy:

■ Troy II: Early Bronze Age (Schliemann's Troy)

■ Troy VI: Late Bronze Age (Dorpfeld's Troy)

□ Troy IX: Greek and Roman Settlements

TIMELINE

CA. **3200** B.C.
The Bronze Age begins in the Aegean region.

CA. **3000–2500** B.C.
People from Asia Minor settle at Troy I.

CA. **2500–2200** B.C.
The town of Troy II lasts until it is destroyed by fire.

CA. **2200–2000** B.C.
The city is rebuilt as Troy III.

CA. **2000–1900** B.C.
Troy IV replaces the previous city.

CA. **1900–1800** B.C.
Troy V replaces the previous city.

CA. **1800–1250** B.C.
Troy VI is built, with a great wall and tower.

CA. **1250–1180** B.C.
Troy VIIa replaces the previous city. It is destroyed by some disaster, probably a war.

CA. **1200** B.C.
According to legend, the Trojan War begins.

CA. **1190** B.C.
According to legend, the Trojan War ends.

CA. **1180–1000** B.C.
The city is rebuilt as Troy VIIb.

CA. **1100** B.C.
Greece's dark age begins.

CA. **1000** B.C.
Troy is possibly abandoned.

CA. **800** B.C.
Homer is born in a Greek colony on the Aegean island of Chios.

CA. **700–300** B.C.
Troy VIII is settled by Greek colonists.

CA. 300–0 B.C.
Troy VIX is built.

CA. A.D. 1–300
Romans settle Troy VIX. Greeks begin to adopt Christianity.

CA. 1400S
The Iliad is among the first classical books printed in Europe.

1816
Danish archaeologist Christian Thomsen names three distinct periods in early human history—the Stone Age, the Bronze Age, and the Iron Age.

1822
Heinrich Schliemann is born in Germany.

1868
Schliemann arrives in the Troad to look for the ruins of Troy.

1869
Schliemann and Sophia Engastromenos marry in Greece.

1870
Without official permission, Schliemann begins the first excavation of the hill at Hissarlik. Turkish government authorities stop the dig.

1871
Schliemann begins the first official excavation of Hissarlik.

1872
Schliemann finds the sun metope, an ancient wall, and other artifacts. He announces to European newspapers that he has found Troy.

1873
Schliemann digs up a mass of gold objects he calls the Treasure of Priam.

1874
The Schliemanns begin excavating Mycenae.

1876
The Schliemanns discover five shaft graves at Mycenae containing the remains of twenty-one Bronze Age people.

1878
Schliemann returns to Troy for another excavation.

1879
Frank Calvert, French archaeologist Emile Burnouf, and German scientist Rudolf Virchow join the dig at Troy.

1882
Schliemann returns to Troy for the third major excavation. German architect Wilhelm Dorpfeld joins him to help identify the ruined buildings. After identifying several major buildings, Schliemann announces that his work at Troy is done.

1884
The Schliemanns and Dorpfeld begin excavations at the ancient Greek city of Tiryns. Schliemann's health is beginning to fail.

1890
After his theories on Troy are challenged by a German critic, Schliemann returns to Troy for another excavation. Late in the year, Schliemann travels alone to Italy, where he dies.

1894
Dorpfeld ends his work at Troy after identifying nine layers of the ruined city.

1932
A team of U.S. archaeologists led by Carl Blegen begins working at Troy. They identify forty-six sublayers of the nine cities.

1945
During World War II, a Russian officer moves some crates containing the Treasure of Priam to Moscow, Russia.

1987
A Russian museum curator discovers the Treasure of Priam in a Moscow government building.

1988
A team of German archaeologists led by Manfred Korfmann begins working at Troy and farther afield in the Troad.

1996
The Treasure of Priam and other pieces from Schliemann's collection are exhibited at the Pushkin Museum in Moscow.

PRONUNCIATION GUIDE

Scholars are unsure what language the Trojans spoke. Most of the stories of Troy come to us through Greek poets. The poets used Greek names for people, places, and gods and goddesses.

Below is a pronunciation key to the personal names and place-names used in the text:

Achaeans	uh-KEE-unz	Heinrich Schliemann	HYN-rihk SHLEE-mahn
Achilles	uh-KIL-eez	Hera	HIHR-uh
Aegean Sea	ih-JEE-uhn	Homer	HO-muhr
Aeneid	ih-NEE-id	*Iliad*	IH-lee-uhd
Agamemnon	a-guh-MEM-nahn	Lysimachus	ly-SIH-muh-kuhs
Ajax	AY-jaks	Menelaus	meh-nuh-LAY-uhs
Andromache	an-DRAH-muh-kee	Mycenae	my-SEE-nee
Aphrodite	a-fruh-DY-tee	Mycenaean	my-SEE-nee-uhn
Apollo	uh-PAHL-oh	Odysseus	oh-DIH-see-uhs
Astyanax	a-STY-uh-nax	*Odyssey*	AH-duh-see
Athena	uh-THEE-nuh	Priam	PRY-uhm
Atreus	ay-TREE-us	Trojans	TROH-junz
Bunarbashi	bun-ahr-BAH-shee	Zeus	ZOOS
Hecuba	HEH-kyuh-buh		

GLOSSARY

acropolis: a fortified city on top of a hill

antiquities: objects, especially works of art, made during ancient times

archaeology: the recovery and study of buildings, tools, pottery, and other objects used by humans in the past

Bronze Age: the period in history when humans relied on tools and weapons made of bronze. In the Aegean area, the Bronze Age lasted from about 3200 to 1100 B.C.

citadel: a fortress—a fortified building or a walled city

Cyclopean: made of very large stone building blocks, as a wall or house. Ancient legends claimed the stone blocks were so large that they were made by a race of giants, the Cyclopes.

Dardanelles: an older British name for the city of Canakkale, Turkey. In modern times, "the Dardanelles" is the Western name for the strait (narrow body of water) connecting the Aegean Sea and the Sea of Marmara. The Greeks called the strait the Hellespont. The strait's modern Turkish name is Canakkale Bogazi.

dark age: a period in history marked by a loss of progress in trade, government, and culture

death mask: a mold made from a person's face after death. Death masks were common around the world into modern times. The death masks found at Mycenae were made of gold. The ancient Greeks may have made wax molds of the dead person's face and then used the molds to make the gold masks.

diadem: a gold or jeweled headband worn as a crown

fortress: a fortified place, such as a building or a walled city

idols: an object that represents a god or goddess, such as a statue

metope (MET-uh-pee): a panel that decorates the top part of the temple, just under the roof

necropolis: a cemetery. In ancient Greek, *necropolis* meant "city of the dead."

pergamus: a city on top of a hill

pithoi: very large storage jars

potsherds: in archaeology, broken bits of ancient pottery

prehistory: the period before humans began keeping written historical records

relief: figures or shapes that are carved to stand out from a surface

shaft grave: a grave formed by a shaft leading to an underground tomb. A shaft, or narrow passage, was dug through the soil. Beneath the shaft, workers dug a large pit to form the tomb. The bodies of the dead and treasures were laid in the tomb. Workers then covered the shaft entrance to the tomb with wood or reeds. The shaft was filled in with dirt.

stelae (*singular* stele): stone slabs, often carved or decorated. Stelae were sometimes used as gravestones.

strata: layers of deposited materials, such as dirt, stones, or building ruins

terra-cotta: a reddish brown clay used to make pottery and other objects

tholos (*plural* tholoi): ancient beehive-shaped building

tumulus (*plural* tumuli): a large mound of earth over a burial spot

WHO'S WHO?

Frank Calvert (1828–1908) was born on Malta, an island in the Mediterranean Sea, to British parents in the Dardanelles. Calvert and his brothers helped British and other Western governments do business in the Turkish-run port city.

In his spare time, Calvert explored the archaeological ruins of the nearby Troad region. He believed that the ruins of Troy could be found at Hissarlik. But he did not have the money to excavate Hissarlik. In the summer of 1868, Calvert met Heinrich Schliemann in the Dardanelles. Hoping that Schliemann would pay to excavate Hissarlik, Calvert shared his theory with him.

If the British Museum had funded Calvert's excavation, he might have gone down in history as the discoverer of Troy. Instead, his name almost disappeared from the record. In 1973 British archaeologist John M. Cook found Calvert's unpublished manuscript on Troad archaeology in the Istanbul Archaeological Museum. These discoveries helped show Calvert's importance to the story of Troy.

Wilhelm Dorpfeld (1853–1940) was a German architect who worked on several archaeological digs in the Aegean region. At that time, archaeologists began hiring architects to help them make sense of the buildings buried under centuries of ruins. In 1882 Dorpfeld was only in his twenties when he was hired to work at the excavations of the ancient city of Olympia. But he quickly gained a good reputation. He was intelligent, organized, and good with the excavation workers.

In 1881 Dorpfeld and Schliemann met at Olympia. The next year, Schliemann convinced Dorpfeld to join him at Troy. Dorpfeld also accompanied the Schliemanns to Tiryns and Mycenae. He is credited with sorting out much of the confusion Schliemann created by digging carelessly at Troy. After Schliemann's death, Dorpfeld continued to work at Homer's lost city, finding evidence of a great war and fire. He identified nine layers to the city, a theory that was confirmed by later archaeologists.

Homer (CA. 800–740 B.C.?) is the author of *The Iliad*, *The Odyssey*, and other poems. Almost nothing is known of Homer's life. Some scholars do not even think there was just one Homer. They believe *The Iliad* and other works were created by several poets over many years. Those works, the scholars think, were finally written down under the name of Homer sometime in the 700s B.C. Other experts say that many things about the poems show they are the work of one person. Those scholars see no reason to doubt that Homer really existed.

Heinrich Schliemann (1822–1890) was born in the town of Neu-Bucknow in Mecklenburg-Schwerin, a region in northern Germany. Heinrich was nine when his mother, Louisa, died. Her death and a scandal involving his father, Ernest, were disastrous for the family. The Schliemann children were separated and sent to live with relatives. After a few years in school, the teenaged Heinrich had to work for a living.

He took a job on a ship bound for South America. But the ship sank in the North Sea, leaving only Schliemann and another survivor. Schliemann literally washed up on the shore of the Netherlands. He got a job with an importing company in the Dutch city of Amsterdam. He worked his way up until he had enough money and contacts to start his own business. From there, he invested in businesses throughout Europe, South America, and North America.

In his spare time, Schliemann continued to study. He took business courses and studied other subjects on his own. He taught himself to speak Dutch, Greek, Italian, Latin, Portuguese, Russian, and Spanish. When he retired from business in his forties, he began to study ancient history and archaeology. After he married Sophia in 1869, the couple immersed themselves in Greek history and archaeology.

He could be arrogant, rude, dishonest, and vain. Like many other Europeans of his day, he disliked and distrusted Turkish people. He loved the ancient Greeks, but he viewed many of the Greeks he knew as ignorant peasants. He failed to credit other archaeologists and experts for their help. And most seriously for modern archaeologists, he had no idea what he was doing when he started work on Troy. He dug straight down for his fabled city, destroying any artifacts that got in his way.

For all his failings, Schliemann remains one of the most important archaeologists of the nineteenth century. His discoveries at Troy and Mycenae opened up a new window into life in the ancient world.

Sophia Engastromenos Schliemann (1852–1932) first met her older German suitor in the early autumn of 1869. She had just graduated from school and lived with her family in Athens. At one of their first meetings, Schliemann asked her why she wanted to marry him. Sophia answered honestly: because her parents told her she had to. Insulted, Schliemann called off the marriage arrangements and left Athens in a huff. Sophia was confused by his reaction. She wrote to him to explain that all good Greek girls obeyed their parents. All was repaired, and the couple married.

Sophia deserves much credit for her attitude in the first years of the marriage. Pretty and delicate, she might have expected to live a life of comfort as the wife of a millionaire. Instead, she often found herself living without heat and running water in shacks built on archaeological sites. She picked bugs out of her food and bathed in the freezing ocean. She dug through ancient debris and dirt in the heavy clothes and tight undergarments women of her day had to wear. Sophia also dealt well with her husband's temper and personality. He lacked the skill to work with government authorities and local workers. He often just insulted and angered them. Sophia stepped in to smooth ruffled feathers.

Sophia did not accompany her husband everywhere. Sometimes she refused to go on digs so she could spend time with her children. And if she got too tired in the middle of an excavation, she returned to the comfort of Athens. But by and large, Sophie took as much pleasure in unearthing Greek history as her husband did.

SOURCE NOTES

8 Leo Deuel, *Memoirs of Heinrich Schliemann* (New York: Harper and Row, 1977), 232.

8 Homer, *The Iliad*, trans. Robert Fagles (New York: Penguin Books, 1990), 81.

8 Ibid., 115.

9 Herve Duchene, *Golden Treasures of Troy: The Dream of Heinrich Schliemann*, trans. Jeremy Leggart (New York: Harry N. Abrams, 1996), 56

13 Schliemann, quoted in Deuel, 149.

13 Homer, 110.

13 Ibid., 217.

15 Heinrich Schliemann, quoted in Deuel, 148.

15 Ibid., 149.

15 Ibid., 150.

17 Ibid., 153.

17 Michael Wood, *In Search of the Trojan War*, rev. ed. (Berkeley: University of California Press, 1996), 55.

18 Schliemann, quoted in Wood, 47.

23 Deuel, 165.

24 Schliemann, quoted in Deuel, 179.

26 Schliemann, quoted in Duchene, 62.

27 Schliemann, quoted in Deuel, 187.

27 Ibid., 188.

27 Ibid., 182.

30 Ibid., 197.

30 Ibid., 198.

30 Ibid.

30 Susan Heuck Allen, *Finding the Walls of Troy* (Berkeley: University of California Press, 1999), 162.

31 Schliemann, quoted in Deuel, 205.

32 Ibid., 206.

32 Wood, 59.

32 Ibid.

32 Allen, 163.

33 Ibid.

40 Deuel, 227.

40 Schliemann, quoted in Deuel, 234.

43 Schliemann, quoted in Wood, 68.

43 Wood, 79.

44 Schliemann, quoted in Deuel, 248.

45 Duchene, 75.

49 Schliemann, quoted in Deuel, 265.

52 Ibid., 269.

52 Wood, 86.

53 Duchene, 92.

54 Schliemann, quoted in Deuel, 292.

54 Deuel, 284.

55 Ibid., 288.

55 Schliemann, quoted in Deuel, 303.

56 Deuel, 311.

58 Duchene, 87.

59 Wood, 89.

61 Wood, 228.

64 Manfred Korfmann, "Was There a Trojan War?" *Archaeology* 57, no. 3 (May/June 2004): 38.

64 Wood, 12.

SELECTED BIBLIOGRAPHY

Allen, Susan Heuck. *Finding the Walls of Troy*. Berkeley: University of California Press, 1999.

Dartmouth College. "Prehistoric Archaeology of the Aegean." *Dartmouth College*. 1997. http://projectsx.dartmouth.edu/history/bronze_age/index.html (July 7, 2007).

Deuel, Leo. *Memoirs of Heinrich Schliemann*. New York: Harper and Row, 1977.

Duchene, Herve. *Golden Treasures of Troy: The Dream of Heinrich Schliemann*. Translated by Jeremy Leggart. New York: Harry N. Abrams, 1996.

Homer. *The Iliad*. Translated by Robert Fagles. New York: Penguin Books, 1990.

Korfmann, Manfred. "Was There a Trojan War?" *Archaeology* 57, no. 3 (May/June 2004): 36–41. Also available online at http://www.archaeology.org/0405/etc/troy.html#homer (January 23, 2008).

Latacz, Joachim. "Evidence from Homer." *Archaeology* 57, no. 3 (May/June 2004): 39. Also available online at http://www.archaeology.org/0405/etc/troy2.html (January 23, 2008).

Rowbotham, William. "Mycenae and the Bronze Age of Greece." *Odyssey: Adventures in Archaeology*. 2002. http://www.odysseyadventures.ca/articles/mycenae/article_mycenae.htm (January 23, 2008).

Wood, Michael. *In Search of the Trojan War*. Rev. ed. Berkeley: University of California Press, 1996.

FURTHER READING AND WEBSITES

BOOKS

Coolidge, Olivia. *The Trojan War*. Boston: Houghton Mifflin, 2001.

Day, Nancy. *Your Travel Guide to Ancient Greece*. Minneapolis: Twenty-First Century Books, 2001.

DiPiazza, Francesca. *Turkey in Pictures*. Minneapolis: Twenty-First Century Books, 2005.

Fontes, Justine, and Ron Fontes. *The Trojan Horse: The Fall of Troy*. Minneapolis: Graphic Universe, 2007.

McGee, Marnie. *National Geographic Investigates: Ancient Greece*. Washington, DC: National Geographic Children's Books, 2006.

McIntosh, Jane. *Archaeology*. New York: DK Eyewitness Books, 2000.

Schlitz, Laura Amy. *The Hero Schliemann: The Dreamer Who Dug for Troy*. Cambridge, MA: Candlewick, 2006.

WEBSITES

Ancient Greece for Kids: The Story of the Trojan War
http://greece.mrdonn.org/trojanwar.html
This website tells the basic story of the Trojan War, with links to more information. Topics include what happened to the Trojan survivors, how Odysseus got home to Ithaca, and life in ancient Greece.

Troia VR: Reconstructions
http://www.uni-tuebingen.de/troia/vr/vr0201_en.html
The website of the Troia Project at the University of Tuebingen in Germany includes some archaeology reconstructions. Houses, fortress walls and ramps, and public buildings from some of Troy's levels are re-created in color.

INDEX

ABOUT THE AUTHOR

Ann Kerns has edited many nonfiction books for young readers and is the author of *Australia in Pictures*, *Romania in Pictures*, and *Martha Stewart*. She enjoys reading, travel, cooking, and music. A native of Illinois, she is a happy transplant to Minneapolis, Minnesota.

PHOTO ACKNOWLEDGMENTS

The images in this book are used with permission of: © Bildarchiv Preussischer Kulturbesitz/Art Resource, NY, pp. 4, 13, 20, 26, 32, 55; © Ancient Art & Architecture Collection, Ltd., p. 6; © Laura Westlund/Independent Picture Service, pp. 9, 65; © Images&Stories/Alamy, pp. 10, 60; © Erich Lessing/Art Resource, NY, pp. 14, 25, 36, 46; The Art Archive, pp. 16-17; Mary Evans Picture Library, p. 22; © akg-images, pp. 28, 31, 48-49, 51, 54; © Mary Evans Picture Library/Alamy, p. 33; © Heinrich Schliemann Papers, Gennadius Library, American School of Classical Studies at Athens, p. 34; © Mansell/Time&Life Pictures/Getty Images, p. 35; © iStockphoto.com/Hulton Archive, p. 39; Library of Congress (LC-USZ62-65911), p. 42; © Nimatallah/Art Resource, NY, p. 43; © akg-images/ Peter Connolly, p. 57; AP Photo/Sergei Karpukhin, p. 62; © Paul Petterson/Art Directors, p. 63.

Front cover: © Bildarchiv Preussischer Kulturbesitz/Art Resource, NY.